# HOW TO

*Market*

A

*Book Release*

## DEVELOP YOUR BEST MARKETING STRATEGY FOR EACH LAUNCH

# Misty M. Beller

ISBN-10: 1547193441
ISBN-13: 978-1547193448

# 1

# Prerequisite: Finding Your Target Reader

It was a dark and stormy night, but the lights shone brightly in Kelly Author's suburban bungalow. A yawn crept through her, breaking her focus on the laptop screen. Lifting her bleary gaze, she raised her arms in a stretch. What she wouldn't do for a bar of chocolate right now. Or maybe a cup of hot tea. The breakfast blend, because she still had so much to do on this manuscript before she turned in for the night.

Refocusing stinging eyes on the monitor, she read the scant plot she'd outlined so far.

**Ryan returns to the university from spring break, but is barely there a week before the trouble starts.**

But what trouble? No matter how many times she started a list of possible plot points, her mind began to wander. But she had to focus here. Book 2 wasn't going to write itself, and she'd promised readers they'd get Ryan's story, the younger brother of her hero from Book 1.

He'd seemed like such a great guy when he'd been Darren's sidekick in the first book. Readers had loved him. But now, the bio she'd created for him reminded her of the cardboard racing star propped up at the hardware store. Flat and obviously not a real person. The setting didn't even seem right. He was supposed to be finishing his sophomore year at the university, but the last thing she wanted to write about was a major university nestled smack dab in the middle of a huge city. It was more than enough that she had to fight Atlanta traffic herself. She sure didn't want to describe pent-up emotions of sitting in rush hour, the choking exhaust fumes, the faceless commuters all stuck in the rat-race.

As if the mouse moved of its own accord, the cursor floated up to her internet browser. Wonder of wonders, the open tab was marked by the Amazon icon, and the sales page for her debut novel stared back at her. Such a familiar site, it sent warm tingles through her chest. So much work she'd put into this story. Then months of editing and tweaking and killing her darlings.

She moved the little white arrow to rest on the row of yellow stars. Ooh, the rating had risen to 4.8. She clicked, completely ignoring the urge to X out of the screen. She knew better than to read reviews, but it was like an addictive drug. Besides, these latest two were both five-star. How much could they hurt?

> ★★★★★ **Loved the Setting**
> By Adventurous Soul
>
> Great story about a guy who treks off to Alaska to become a hunting guide. Loved the action, and especially the remote setting! I live in Colorado and love the mountains, but this book made me wanna move to Alaska. Keep writing and I'll keep reading...

Yep, she loved the Alaskan wilderness setting, too. It was one of the things that made that book so much fun to write. She skimmed down to the next new review.

> ★★★★★ **Transported me**
> By Book Reader
>
> This is my favorite kind of book, where the author transports me into a totally different place and I get to experience all those new things. And this book kept you on your toes! If you love adventure and wilderness life, you'll love this story. Ready for book 2!

Hmm... Both reviews mentioned adventure and the wilderness setting. Well, they were going to be sadly disappointed when they read Ryan's story.

But...why did they have to be?

Her pulse thrummed in her ears as her adrenaline took charge. She called up the half-filled white page, then positioned her fingers on the keyboard and started typing.

The storyline spewed onto the screen as images flashed through her mind. Ryan and his buddy spent the last few weeks of school planning the trip of a lifetime, hitting the top five most thrilling sites in Canada. Yep,

Canada.

They'd be ziplining through the Whistler and Blackcomb mountains, biking part of the Trans Canada Trail, rafting the Shubenacadie tidal bore, and if they made it all the way to the West Coast, they'd kayak with the killer whales. But neither of the guys planned for the mysterious woman who dogs their trail from the moment they cross the border at Niagara Falls. Nor do they allot time in the schedule for the murder Ryan is almost certain he witnessed. Or did he?

Kelly leaned back from the computer, cupping the stress ball in her hands as she rereads her notes. Yes, this is exactly the kind of story those reviewers will love. She could just imagine Adventurous Soul perched in the recliner of her Colorado chalet, following Ryan's exploits and urging him to search harder for the woman after he thinks she was pushed over the cliff to her death.

Yep, not only did she know what she was going to write, she also knew exactly who was going to read it— and love every word.

\* \* \* \* \*

## Who is *your* target reader?

The more I delve into marketing and ways to find new readers, the more important it's become for me to understand who my target reader is. What kind of people tend to fall in love with my books? (Not just those who can tolerate them.) Where do I find those people?

I know I promised a book on all the best methods to market your new release, but so many of the most important strategies **require** you to know who your target reader is, or else your time and resources will be wasted.

The deeper I go in this topic, the more I'm intrigued by it. The more I understand the freeing power of knowing my target reader, the more it influences my story lines, the types of characters I write about, the settings in each book, my book covers, back cover blurbs, types of advertising, you name it!

***Good marketing starts with knowing who you want to reach.***

In other words, almost everything I do related to books centers around my target reader—making sure they can find my book, and then making sure they love it!

So how do you find that elusive person?

Is it a demographic (for example, women from ages 35-60)? I'm going to push you to go deeper than that. Is it a lifestyle? How can you possibly know?

It's possible that each author comes to their understanding differently, but I'll share some tips that might help you take a more direct route to your "ah-ha" moment.

**Technique #1: What stirs emotions in you?**

This technique works best if you write the kind of books you love to read (and in general, I'd recommend that you do write in the genre you enjoy reading). If, for example, you're a 50-year-old writing middle grade (children's) books, you might try asking a middle grade student what they enjoy most about the books they read.

Also, this technique works for both pre-published and published writers.

Think about a location or setting that stirs you. What ignites a spark in your soul? Maybe it gives you a warm and fuzzy feeling, a yearning, or makes your pulse race.

For me, I love mountain settings. The beauty…the majesty. Standing on the edge of a peak looking out for miles and miles…I come alive in a way that's almost intoxicating. And my favorite season in the mountains is winter, when snow paints the landscape in sparkling layers. Some of my happiest times have been spent in a mountain cabin, hiding away from the world as the snow covers the peaks in a soft blanket of white. Just thinking about it fills me with an intense craving to be there.

That, my friends, is a setting that stirs me. It stirs a whole audience of people. I can write with passion, helping others experience the same gamut of emotion that I experience when I imagine those scenes.

## Technique #2: What do people talk about when they post a review?

If you already have a book published, read through your Amazon reviews, looking for consistent themes. What did people love about this book? Was it the hero's tragic past, and how he learns to forgive himself? Was it the fact that heroine came from a wealthy upbringing, yet had the tenacity to learn the skills needed to survive in a wild, barren country?

Find those themes and drill into them. Then, weave those same elements into future books. Chances are, they are also characteristics that drew you to your hero and heroine to begin with.

These will become elements of your brand as an author.

In my writing, I've found my target reader loves strong, brooding heroes, usually the silent type. My people enjoy heroines who come from culture and class, whether they were born to it or found it through unusual ways. My readers love to see how these aristocratic heroines learn to adjust and embrace the wild beauty of the west, and learn to love it so much they never want to leave.

**Technique #3: Use Facebook Ad targeting to discover more about your target readers.**

This method was a bit of a surprise for me. If you've not used FB ads before, they allow you to target people based on things they've shown an interest in. For example, you can target well-known authors, publishing houses, interest groups, locations, etc.

As I tested several audience types with various interests, I found some common themes among the groups that resulted in the lowest cost-per-click for my ads. Those groups had shown interest in Janette Oke, the Love Comes Softly series, Hallmark movies, and Bethany House Publishers. Are you hearing a theme?

Additionally, Facebook shows you cost-per-click breakdown by age range and gender. I found my lowest cost-per-click with women in the 45 – 65+ range. That didn't surprise me, but it did surprise me that I paid almost twice as much for any click outside of that demographic. Hmm...

My favorite type of Facebook ad when I'm looking for new specifics in my audience is Lead Generation ads. These function differently than "normal" ads, but they tend to be my most helpful tool to identify the interests of my target reader. I've written a "how-to" blog post that walks through the set-up of Facebook Lead Generation ads[1].

---

### TRAD-PUBed TIPS

*Once you clearly articulate the type of reader who loves your books, ask your publisher's team to help translate those details into a cover and back cover blurb that will delight your audience.*

*And remember, if you've done your research, you should know your target reader better than anyone by now. Don't be afraid to follow your instincts in these conversations.*

---

[1]https://theambitiousauthor.com/2017/04/24/why-i-love-facebook-lead-generation-ads/

### INDIE INSIGHTS

*Indie authors have the unique ability to respond quickly to the needs and desires of your target reader. If you realize that some of your covers don't resonate with your target reader, change those covers!*

*In your book blurbs, make sure you highlight the things that will draw your target reader. And don't be afraid to rewrite until you find the perfect fit.*

*Indie publishing allows you to be agile and respond to the needs and desires of your target reader. Figure out what delights that person, then use that understanding to focus your stories, covers, blurbs, etc.*

*You'll come to treasure that connection with lifetime readers!*

## Homework:

If you don't already have a strong connection with your target reader, take the time now to discover them. There's nothing quite as special as a kindred spirit!

**Write at least three sentences describing your target reader.**

Go deeper than demographics. Tell us what settings they enjoy, or perhaps types of characters. Tell us names of other authors your reader can't get enough of. Are there particular sports or vacations they enjoy? Start brainstorming and keep asking questions about that person until you feel like you can see them across the table at the coffee shop!

# 2

# A Word About Preorders

Kelly could hardly believe an entire month had passed since that fateful night she discovered her target reader. But what a month.

She'd made it well past the midpoint, almost to the dark moment where Ryan realizes he loves Samantha, the woman who had been pushed over the cliff. (It was a good thing she'd been harnessed to her belay rope and her mountain climbing partner was savvy enough to save her life.)

Readers were going to love the story. She could feel it in her bones.

Her eyes found the calendar mounted on the wall. Three more months until the tentative release date she'd set for herself, but there was so much to do in those months. The book would be ready, she was pretty sure about that. The editor had her slotted in his schedule. Her cover artist had already sent the semi-final design, and was making the final tweaks before working on the print cover design.

And the readers on her email list and social media connections were chomping at the bit to read the story.

Especially since she'd been feeding them tidbits of the manuscript and fun teasers about the story.

Too bad they couldn't buy the book now while their excitement stirred. Sort of that impulse buy the retailers at the mall worked so hard to capture. Hopefully, their interest would remain high for three more months until the official release day came.

But…why did they have to wait?

Leaning over the computer, she popped up the web browser and navigated to the eBook distributor's Terms page. Yep, there it was. A 90-day preorder.

Exactly what she needed to capture those eager readers now while she finished up the final pieces to make this book her best yet.

* * * * *

Just like Kelly, I'm a fan of preorders. For Indie or Small Press authors, it may sometimes be hard to pull everything together—especially a book cover—three months before the actual release date, but in my opinion, it's worth the effort.

Not all traditionally published authors have this option, but in most instances, I recommend making your book available for preorder. A few of the main reasons are:

- It gives you a link to use as you prepare your marketing efforts, including blog posts.
- It extends the productive sale time, growing word of

mouth enthusiasm and giving potential readers the ability to make that quick impulse buy, even before you're ready to release the book.

- You can put the link/book cover/blurb/etc. in the back of your other books so readers are more likely to make an impulse buy when they finish your previous books—again, you're capturing sales even before you're ready to release the book.

These are all great reasons, and allow you to capture sales while you're still finalizing the book content.

But one of my favorite reasons for using preorders is the effect on early reviews. These reader reviews will start to trickle in over the first two weeks after release, and will have that lovely 'verified purchase' stamp on Amazon. It's almost like having a second launch team!

---

### TRAD-PUBed TIPS

*Make the preorder discussion part of the conversation as early as possible. At the time of contract or right after would be ideal! That way, the publisher understands your desire and can work that into the production schedule, if possible.*

---

## Amazon Requirements

Before we go further on the topic, though, let me call out a few details that will be helpful during our discussion. The larger traditional publishing houses can negotiate some of these requirements, but for the rest of us, this is how it works on Amazon, specifically. Other retailer's requirements vary a little.

1.  You're allowed to release a title for pre-order up to 90 days before the actual release date. At any time during the pre-order period, you can move the release date up (make it June 15th instead of June 30th), but you may NOT push it out (make it July 5th instead of June 30th).

2.  When readers purchase a pre-order book, they are given a price guarantee. If the price drops at any time during the pre-order period, they are charged the lesser price. This means if you lower your pre-order price half way through the period, ALL pre-order sales will be sold at that lesser price.

3.  You are required to submit the basic book information before you can make the pre-order live. Amazon requires you to upload a manuscript file, but you tell them whether it's the final draft or not. Interestingly, whether you say it's the final draft or not, you are allowed to upload a new draft at any time until about 3 days before the official release date.

4.  The pre-orders all dump into your KDP Reports (and into Amazon's system as actual sales) on the evening BEFORE your release. This is very important to one of the benefits we'll talk about shortly!

**A few more reasons I like preorders...**

5. **Early Reviews!** Most authors have lamented the fact that reviews can't be posted on Amazon.com until the book is officially released. I've developed a bit of a loop-hole to help with this. While the eBook is available for pre-order with the strict release date I've chosen, I release my paperback version a couple days before. That way, my launch team and early reviewers can click the Paperback version and leave their review, but all my eBook sales can stick to the release date I've chosen.

6. **Bestseller lists!** This won't apply to everyone, but if you're planning a strategy to hit one of the bestseller lists (like *USA Today*), pre-orders are an absolute must. Keep in mind, though, that the sales all register the day BEFORE your release date. So, if the list you're targeting tracks sales from Monday to Sunday, set your actual release date as a Tuesday because most of the preorder sales will become *actual* sales on the day before (Monday).

7. **Cover art...** For most people, cover art is one of the last steps in the pre-publishing process. If you use pre-orders, you'll need to rearrange the order of your process a little. I've actually started creating my cover art fairly early in my writing process, partly due to my use of pre-order for the full 90 days. It's had a pleasant side effect that I can also make sure my character and location descriptions in the story match what I've chosen for the cover. Win-win!

## INDIE INSIGHTS

*One of the best things about being an indie author is being able to choose the right path for you and your books! So, are preorders right for you?*

*Preorder might be a great option for you if...*

*• you can decently stick to a deadline, even if you're a procrastinator.*
*• you're pretty close to the end of your pre-publishing process.*
*• you want to increase your number of reviews within the first few weeks of releasing.*
*• you're working to sell enough books to boost your title onto a bestseller list.*

*You will need to be careful with the pre-order strategy and plan effectively if...*

*• you can't meet a deadline to save your soul.*
*• you have a specific reason the cover art can't be created earlier in the process.*

# 3

# New vs. Existing Readers: Reaching Both

The deed was done.

Kelly stared at the pop-up box that confirmed her book's preorder availability. If she had to describe the emotions coursing through her, in a first draft she would say exhilaration mixed with a bit of apprehension—or maybe downright fear. But after she'd edited out the telling words, she might describe the sensations as her pulse thumping a staccato beat through her chest, her palms a little damp, and she had to draw a long breath to steady herself.

She was doing this. Releasing her baby into the world. It wasn't quite grown yet, but the date had been secured. June 27th.

Another breath.

She now had a purchase link, it was time to get the word out about her new release. Time to get herself organized. Make a plan.

Grabbing her notebook and pencil, she curled her legs underneath her and stared at the pastel lines spanning the otherwise empty page. Where to start?

She definitely wanted to reach the people who read book one in the series. Too bad she'd waited several months after the book's release to start her email list. Her social media posts seemed to be seen by fewer and fewer people these days. But she'd definitely use all the weapons in her arsenal.

But she wanted this book to reach new readers, too. After all, she'd made the story so that it could be read as a standalone. And hopefully readers who began the series with book two would circle back to book one, as well. So how to reach those new readers?

Turning the page sideways, she drew two circles side-by-side on the paper. In the first, she wrote "Existing Readers" and in the second, "New Readers." Then she drew circles out from each of those like spokes on wheels as her mind began to spin...

\* \* \* \* \*

In its simplest form, you're either selling books to Existing Readers or New Readers. So, as we prepare to launch a new book, you want to make sure you're targeting both groups. If this is your debut, don't skip this next section! For your first release, all your marketing efforts will be to New Readers, but you want to make sure you have systems in place to reach those Existing Readers on your next launch.

Here's a little graphic I like to use to visualize the outreach:

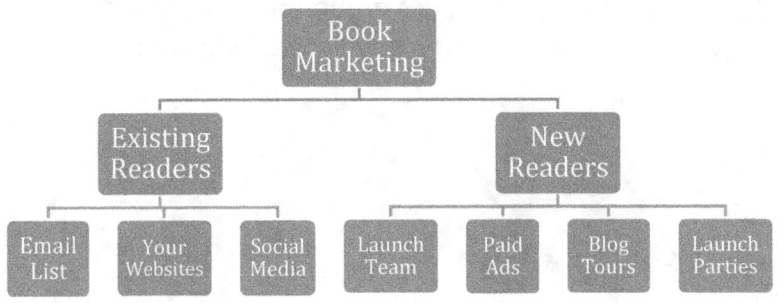

## Homework:

Think about a recent book launch. If you're published, use your most recent release. If you're not yet published, either use a marketing plan you've put together for a proposal or think of another author's book launch that you are familiar with. If you don't have any of these, just make up some things you think you would do for your first book release.

Make a quick list of the top 5-10 things you did or would do for the book release. Your list could look like this:

- Post link and excerpt from book on my Facebook Author Page.
- Write guest posts for ten blogs that reach my target reader.
- Etc.

Now separate the items on your list into two categories according to which audience they will reach: New Readers or Existing Readers.

Don't skip that last step! It's important you train yourself to be cognizant of which target group each marketing activity will touch so you make sure you're reaching both.

# 4

# Tool #1: Email List

Kelly's pencil hovered over the circle marked "Existing Readers." Where to start?

A soft ding sounded from her phone, pulling her focus away from the paper. Better turn down the volume so she wasn't distracted. But as she picked up the device, an email flashed across the home screen. The subject line showed the message came through the contact form on her website, so she pressed the unlock button to read the content.

Ms. Author,

I just had to tell you how much I LOVEDDDDDD Darren's story! I felt like I was there with him in the Alaskan wilderness the entire time! I can't wait for the next book in the series! Do you know when it will be release? I signed up for your new release alerts, but I haven't seen anything yet. Please hurry! I'm dying to read Ryan's story!!! ☺

Sincerely,

Your biggest fan

Kelly did a little bounce in her chair as her eyes roamed back over the message. Her biggest fan. And she was dying to read Ryan's story. How happy this fan would be to hear that Ryan's story was available now for preorder purchase!

Moving back to her marketing diagram, she went straight to the first circle extending from the "Existing Readers" and penciled "Send email to mailing list."

After all, she'd promised those who signed up would be first to hear about new releases.

\* \* \* \* \*

As you grow your email list, this will become one of your most helpful tools in a book launch. So let's dive in!

First, if you haven't started your email list yet, DO NOT BE AFRAID OF IT! This is essentially a list of your readers, people who have requested to hear from you about your book updates. That's a great thing!

**When and How to Start Your List**

I encourage people to create their email list from the first moment they know their book is going to be published. If you're going the traditional publisher route, start your list when you sign that contract. If you plan to indie publish, start your list as soon as you make the decision to pursue that route. Even when you're in those pre-published stages, a formal email list helps you gather info from interested people, and the software keeps that info safe and organized until you're ready to announce your new release!

So how to start? You want to use a professional service, not an Excel spreadsheet that you manage yourself. Other than the obvious administrative work, anti-spam laws are very specific in most countries about what is required when you send emails to a subscriber. The professional services will keep you legal.

Many of the reputable email list services allow you to use them at no charge until your email list exceeds 1,000 or 2,000 subscribers, so there's no reason not to!

A few of the more popular services are Mailchimp, Mailer Lite, and Mad Mimi. Take a look at several providers and see which is the best fit for you.

As you're going through the set-up process, your chosen provider will give you the capability to create a sign-up form that links directly to your email list. Make sure you add that form to your website, your social media pages, and as a link in the back of your existing books.

### *INDIE INSIGHTS*

*A great benefit of being indie is the ability to keep the back matter of all your books updated with your current booklist. You find a significant part of your sales and quality email sign-ups come from the back matter.*

*If you use a professional formatter, make sure you have access to update the files any time you wish without incurring a lot of additional expense!*

### *TRAD-PUBed TIPS*

*Publishers understand the value of an author email list, so don't be afraid to ask if they will include a link for readers to sign-up for your email list in the back matter of your books. They may have a valid reason to say no, but at least you asked.*

*If they do agree to include the sign-up link, create a free account with a link shortening software such as bit.ly or tinyurl.com. With those services, you can change the original link at any time (for example, if you move to a different email list provider) without needing to update the link in the back of the book.*

In your sign-up form, **make sure you're clear about what readers are signing up for**. If you plan to only share new book releases, say that. If you'll send a monthly or quarterly newsletter, say that.

For me personally, I send emails when I have a new release. The note in the back of my eBooks reads: *To get updates when new Misty M. Beller books release, tap here.*

Whatever your plan, make sure you are clear about what you're promising, then you follow through on that promise.

**So how do you grow your email list?**

As this topic explodes through the author world, we're finding options for growth pop-up through some unexpected ways. Keep your eyes open!

I'll cover some of those trends here, as well as the tried-and-true methods for growing your reader email list.

No matter your approach(es) to list growth, make sure you're focusing on finding your **target readers**. People who love to read the kind of books you write.

So without further ado, here are my favorite list growth methods:

1. **Organic sign-ups:** This would include having a sign-up form on your website and in the back matter of your books. These are people who have read your stories and desperately want to know when your next book will release! These people tend to give the highest open and click rates on your mailing list.

2. **Give away a piece of your writing to existing readers** (on your website and in the backs of your books.) This is an extra incentive for people who read your work, a little more encouragement for them to join your list.

The incentive could be:

- Short story or novella
- A prequel or story between your books
- Christmas or other holiday story involving the same characters
- Behind the scenes of your writing process
- Character sketches
- Anything that will attract people who like what you write!

The incentive I offer is a short story following one of my most popular series. It's the birth story of the hero in *The Lady and the Mountain Call*, and shares the emotional tale of his adoption.

No matter what incentive you choose, make sure it's your own writing and will be attractive to your target reader.

A final word on the logistics of giving away an incentive like this: You can use a paid service that creates a giveaway page where you direct readers (like BookFunnel's mid-level plan or Instafreebie's paid version). Or you can set it up yourself so the giveaway runs on autopilot (and free) using your email list service provider (like Mailchimp) combined with BookFunnel's free level.

I've had so many people ask me about this, I created a free 20-minute video course that shows you each step[2].

3. **Monthly drawing for a book in the same genre you write**. I've done this a few times, and have heard of authors who love this option. Just be careful to make sure the books you give away draw your target reader.

4. **Group Giveaways.** The power of group giveaways lies in the fact that all authors are promoting the giveaway to their respective email list and social media platforms.

Currently, I've seen two versions of these:

1. Giveaways where multiple authors come together to form a larger giveaway of one book from each author, along with another prize like a Kindle. An example of this is the giveaways coordinated by ryanzee.com. Each author only needs to provide a couple copies of their book to the winner and runner-up, and they receive a list of email addresses from readers who have requested to be added to that specific author's email list.

2. Another version of the group giveaway is where each author gives a free copy of their book to *every* reader who signs up for that author's mailing list. Often, these are coordinated by the

---

[2] https://theambitiousauthor.com/free-ecourse-easy-email-list-giveaway/

authors themselves. I've participated in this type of group giveaway using several popular platforms, including Instafreebie, BookFunnel, and My Book Cave.

In general, group giveaways can be very helpful in finding new people who fit your target reader. The unsubscribe rate can be a little higher for readers who come to your list through a group giveaway, as you weed through the list to find those who are actually interested in your books.

I strongly recommend using an automation sequence when onboarding subscribers gained through a giveaway. I find this series of emails is very important in converting new readers to fans and teaching them to buy my books (instead of just hanging around for freebies). You can set this up so each email sends automatically at the frequency you determine.

Here's what my email sequence looks like:

1. Email #1: Immediately sends them the free book they requested and introduces them to me and what I write. It's also helpful to remind readers how they signed up for your list.

2. Email #2: Sent a week after the first email, I ask if they enjoyed the book, then tell them about book 2 in the series, including buy links for the retailers and the first two pages as a teaser.

3. Email #3: Sent a week after the second email, in this final message I tell the reader about my newest release (since I promised to share new release alerts), along with buy links to the retailers.

If you have a book (novella length or longer) you can give away to each subscriber, the following are good options to grow your subscriber list:

- **Facebook ads** for a free book or story you wrote. There are two ad options for this:
  - An ad optimized for website clicks to a landing page where readers receive your free book. This is the same ad set-up you would use to sell books, and I've created a short blog tutorial to walk through the steps[3].
  - Lead Generation ads. I like this version because Facebook makes it simple for users to sign-up without a lot of steps. Another advantage to Lead Gen ads are that Facebook currently allows a $2/day minimum spend for these ads (most other ad types are $5/day minimum spend). This allows you to test different interests and audiences until you find the right fit for your giveaway. I've had good success using Lead Gen ads to find my target audience, then used that audience for sales ads later. Because the set-up is different from most ad types, I created a short blog tutorial to show the steps[4].

- **Giveaways through InstaFreebie** (not part of group giveaways). The Instafreebie website has a wide base of readers who regularly browse the site to discover new authors. Authors can post a book or book excerpt to give

---

[3] https://theambitiousauthor.com/2015/09/29/facebook-ads-demystified/

[4] https://theambitiousauthor.com/2017/04/24/why-i-love-facebook-lead-generation-ads/

away in exchange for the reader's subscription to the author's mailing list. On any given day, I average about a dozen sign-ups for my permafree book that I posted here. The site integrates with my Mailchimp list, so other than paying $20/month, I don't need to do anything further.

## Final notes about growing your email list

When you use many of the giveaways I've listed above to grow your mailing list, there's one additional idea to consider. Because people are signing up for your mailing list (cold) without having actually read your writing, the open and click rates for these readers on your list usually won't be as high as those from organic sign-ups. That's one of the reasons it's so important for all of your branding, including the look and wording on your ads, to have the same consistency. Potential readers should get an immediate feel for your style no matter how they find you! And don't forget the automation sequence I mentioned.

Finally, remember that growing your mailing list takes time and consistency! Some of these strategies allow for faster growth than in the past, but growing your list still requires you to be intentional and consistent. Don't be disappointed if you're not at 10,000 emails within six months.

## Best Practices to Use Your Email List for a Book Launch

As soon as your book is available for sale (hopefully for

preorder!), you want to send an announcement email to your list. Most likely, when you invited people to join your email list, you told them they would be the first to hear about your new releases, so make sure you follow through on that promise!

*Send the announcement to your email list BEFORE you post it on your website or social media.*

I recommend sending three emails during a book launch:

- Email announcing pre-order. Make sure you include buy links for all the retailers. I've also had readers email me requesting that I add UK and Canadian links. And if you're running a special preorder sale price, mention it!
- Email on release day. A fun way to provide added value to people on your list would be to include a special tidbit about your characters or an excerpt from the book. Or maybe you could include the pictures that inspired the appearance of your main characters. Make it fun!
- Send a final email several weeks after the release thanking them for purchasing the book (yes, make the assumption they purchased), tell them you hope they enjoy the story, and encourage them to post a review at their purchase site and Goodreads.

## Homework

What is one thing you can do *right now* to grow your list of reader emails? Maybe it's signing up for a mail service, making a list of possible short stories you could write as a giveaway, or creating a FB Lead Gen ad.

Now go do it!

# 5

# Tool #2: Your Websites

Kelly's pen hovered over the next empty circle. After her email list heard about the new book, she needed to make sure it was posted on her website. And for that matter, her Amazon author page. She'd heard the books didn't always update there automatically. The same for Goodreads.

As more websites popped into her mind, she listed them out. Her BookBub author page, for sure, and she should add the link to her email signature for when she responded to reader emails. Wow, so many ways to get the word out to readers with only a one-time update!

\* \* \* \* \*

Once you've announced your new book to your email list, it's time to get it posted and linked to all your public websites. This includes, but isn't limited to:

- **Your author website.**

- **Amazon author page**. Books aren't always

automatically added to your Amazon author page, so make sure you check each book as soon as it's available. This is also a great time to make sure your bio is updated.

- **BookBub author page**. You've created one right? This is a free service BB offers, and readers can follow your BookBub author page to receive a notice every time you release a new book. This is free, so by all means, utilize it!

- **Goodreads author profile**. If you or your publisher doesn't create the page for each new book, one of your readers will. And that leaves a greater chance that the information won't be accurate. Own your web presence, especially where readers are!

- **Back links of your other books.** If you're an indie author, you can update the back links of your previously published books at any time, so make sure you add your new book as soon as possible! This will be one of your number one methods for early sales.

- **Anywhere** readers will be looking for it, especially if they'll receive notifications!

> **TRAD-PUBed TIPS**
>
> *Ask your publisher for a list of websites where they plan to post the book, so you don't duplicate efforts. It's one of the great benefits of working with a team!*

You'll notice I haven't mentioned any social media platforms yet, but that's coming next.

## Homework

Start a list on your computer or in a favorite notebook of all the websites where you need to post each new book. Include any genre-specific sites and those offered through groups with which you're associated. And if you show book covers on your social media headers, make sure you include those on the list.

# 6

# Tool #3: Social Media Sharing

Kelly's mind raced as she exhausted the list of websites where she would post the new release. No matter what, she couldn't forget to share it on social media. Her friends had suffered through her highs and lows during the writing, so they would surely want to know about the new release. After all, not everyone was into email lists. She would post on Facebook for sure, and she could do some fun things with her new book cover to post on Instagram. And Twitter—she'd met a few people on that network who really seemed to like its quirky platform. Maybe she could get some viral sharing if she made her messages interesting.

So what would encourage people to read and share her posts? She could pull out some fun quotes from the book and create memes with pictures of some of the amazing scenery she described in the book's setting. Those were always a hit, so she wrote it inside one of her bubbles on the chart. But surely she could think of something even more creative. Maybe a video? A book trailer? Maybe...although she'd heard those could get expensive or take up a lot of time. What about if she made a video of herself telling a story from the book? Or a funny moment? She could talk about her aha moment when she realized this was the book she really wanted to write, and how the setting and adventure spoke to her soul. Her pulse picked up speed as she imagined what she would say. If she could share at least a little of the excitement burning inside her, people couldn't help but be affected.

\* \* \* \* \*

It's been a long-undisputed fact that word of mouth sells books. And social media is still king when it comes to spreading word of mouth like wildfire.

Gone are the days when having 1,000 'likes' on your Facebook page would result in at least half that many sales. Not because those people who click the thumbs up on your page don't really want to buy your books, but because the majority of them likely won't see your post.

Yet still, social media should play at least a small part in every book launch, because it's the socially accepted place for people to share what excites them!

As you plan your book launch, I recommend posting at least the same quantity and approximate timing as you send to your email list, making sure you send the email announcement first.

- Post #1: After you announce the new book to your email list, post the link on Facebook, Twitter, Instagram, or whatever platforms you utilize. If you've created a Pinterest board of image inspirations as you were writing the book, clean up the text that accompanies the pictures and make that board public. Make sure you add your book cover linking to Amazon!
- Post #2: On release day, announce it to anyone who will listen!
- Post #3: A few weeks after release, gently encourage readers to post a review. There are so many subtle ways to do this, including highlighting a review you love or posting a cute meme about how much reviews help authors.

One way to help make your posts shareable is to create memes that capture people's attention. Basically, a meme is a picture with words added. There are some great programs that make these easy, including Canva.com, Picmonkey.com, and plain ol' Power Point. As you're creating memes, try to limit the amount of text you use, and make sure the images and words resonate with your target reader. (You knew I would say that somewhere, right?)

### INDIE INSIGHTS

*Often, a cover designer will throw in a meme or two for a few extra dollars when they're creating the cover art for your book. This is a great way to get a professional-looking meme for a cheap price!*

Social media is a great way to let your creativity stretch its legs, as new tools and options continue to unfold. Videos have recently taken hold as people realize the impact of both hearing and seeing a message at the same time. Along those same lines, several social media sites have developed "live" capabilities (e.g. Facebook Live) where you can use your smart phone or laptop camera to interact with friends. This can be a great opportunity to share your enthusiasm about a new release!

Keep in mind that different demographics often have their own preference of communication styles, so learn what your audience prefers: memes, a 'letter' from you, pictures from your writing life, 'live' videos, etc.

And most of all, make sure your communications follow your own unique style—that author 'voice' you've developed through your writing.

## Homework

Make a list of at least five fun ideas you've done or seen another author do to share about a new release on social media. Now beside each of those five, brainstorm ideas to tailor that strategy for your book and make the effect even better!

# 7

# Tool #4: Launch Team

Kelly sank back in her chair, her eyes burning from the strain of brainstorming so feverishly. But she had good stuff here. A solid to-do list. Now she just needed to add some bubbles for the "New Readers" section.

She closed her eyes, thinking through all the advice her author friends had given in the past. Everyone says word of mouth is the best way to sell books. But how could she get people talking? It had to be more than just her touting her own book. She needed a team. People who would read the book—and hopefully enjoy it—then tell others how great the story is.

A Launch Team…

\* \* \* \* \*

This is one of my top three tools in any launch and it's the first we'll discuss that is primarily intended to connect your books with New Readers. Remember that chart I showed you before?

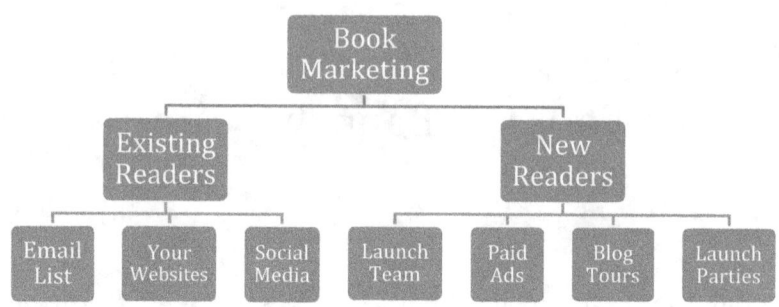

## What is a launch team?

They can be called by many names (street team, fan club, and more), but a launch team is basically a group of readers who are ready and willing (and eager!) to get the word out on the street about an author's books. When I think of my launch team, I think of my first readers, my inside circle, my front lines, my most enthusiastic fans.

## What does a launch team do?

Members are given ARC copies and asked to read the book before release. From there, the role may vary depending on the author and team members, but the common theme and single most important job of a launch team member is to post reviews—on Amazon, Goodreads, and anywhere else the book is available! Reviews help jump-start both Amazon's algorithms and reader confidence in a book, so I work hard to help my books gain at least twenty-five reviews within the first few weeks.

### TRAD-PUBed TIPS

*Your publisher probably already has a standard format for distributing ARCs. Some larger publishers send paperback copies directly to those on your launch team, and only need you to provide names and addresses for each person.*

*Other publishers will provide you with a PDF or eBook files to distribute to your team. Still others use services like NetGalley to send out ARCs.*

*Make sure you know what your publisher is planning and what they need from you, BEFORE you contact your launch team about a new release.*

Beyond reviews, some ideas for the launch team are to:

- Talk about the books on social media sites.
- Blog about the books.
- Direct people to author's website.
- Write a review for their local newspaper.
- Purchase copies to give away as Christmas and birthday gifts.
- Pin the cover and book memes to Pinterest.
- Share favorite quotes from the book on social media.
- Suggest the book on reading forums, like those on Goodreads.

- Like and share the book trailer on YouTube or Vimeo.
- Donate a copy to a local library or church library.
- Suggest the author's latest book to a book club.
- And the list can go on!

## Who makes a great launch team member?

Readers who have read and are excited about the author's books, and want to share that excitement within their sphere of influence. Enthusiasm trumps all. Time availability is important, too!

### *INDIE INSIGHTS*

*There are great FREE programs out there to help authors convert and distribute ARC files in formats that make it easy for your launch team members to read. Calibre is a useful (free) software to convert a Word document to mobi files (for Kindles) and epub files (for iBooks, Nook, and most other ereaders).*

*BookFunnel.com is a helpful resource to distribute the ereader files to your team. It makes the process to download the file onto their ereader as simple as possible, and BookFunnel's customer service is top notch.*

A word of caution, authors tend to lean toward asking other authors to be on their launch team. After all, only a compatriot would understand the importance of the role, right? In my experience, readers tend to be more enthusiastic launch team members, eagerly reading the book and posting reviews as soon as possible. While it's certainly fine to have both, when I open my launch team to new members, I try to post the memo where my readers will see it.

## So how do you find launch team members?

I recommend having a form on your website that asks basic questions, such as what genres the potential candidate likes to read, and whether they've read any of your books already. You could also go one step further and ask for the link to one of the reviews they've posted for your books. How much or how little is your choice!

You can see an example form at my website[5]. When I was actively seeking to grow my team, this page was front and center on my site menu. Now, I have it tucked in as part of the 'About' page so it can be found by readers who are really interested.

Once you have that form in place, you can direct people there from a variety of places:

- Call-out on social media.
- Post the request on your blog.
- Send an email to your list. (Another advantage of

---

[5] http://mistymbeller.com/join-my-launch-team.html

growing your reader list! Just make sure you screen respondents to find those who really want to help with your launches, not just receive free books.)

- A note in the back of your eBooks, if you're feeling ambitious!

**What should you give your launch team in return for their help?**

Free ARCs (advance reader copies) are a given. Beyond that, have fun with it! Here are some fun freebies to share with your team, if you have the opportunity and/or means:

- Insider info, such as the first opportunity to see cover art for your upcoming releases.
- Let them help name characters or choose settings.
- I like to give my team the choice to receive either eBook or paperback copies (signed with a note to them).
- Book swag created for your author brand, such as bookmarks, mugs printed with your book cover, etc.
- Christmas ornaments engraved with your author or book name. Etsy.com has some creative options here!
- Generally speaking, the more you connect with your team, the more they'll want to promote your books.

A word of caution above, Amazon's review requirements are strict about giving gifts in exchange for reviews, so you'll want to be careful to avoid any language about 'requiring reviews' in exchange for any of the benefits received by being on your launch team.

## Make it easy to share your book on social media

People are more likely to share your book when you make it easy for them! There are a couple of ways you can do this:

- The simplest way is to create several Twitter and Facebook posts that people can copy and post to their respective accounts. (Make sure you include a buy link for your book!) You can simply include these in an email to your launch team, or paste them on a Word document you send out.
- A more sophisticated method would be to create a share page on your website. Using a tool like sharelinkgenerator.com, you can create prewritten posts where people only need to click to post your message on any of the social media platforms you include. You can even add memes or other images for easy posting. People are more likely to share your message when you make it possible with only a click or two.

## Tips on Interacting with your Launch Team

- Know your goals for the team and be clear up front about expectations. Do you want them to focus on reviews only, or is social media sharing important to you?
- Send ARCs to your team at least 2-3 months before release, or as early as possible.
- Include links for where to post reviews in your emails to your list. Don't forget Goodreads!

- Even if you haven't made a big deal about your team sharing on social media, make it easy for those who choose to do so!

## Homework

Do you have a launch team and are you satisfied with the size and team members?

If yes, what is one new thing you can do on your next launch to help your team support the new release?

If you answered no to the question above, what is one step you can take to grow your team?

Now go do it!

# 8

# Tool #5: Paid Advertising

With her launch team spreading the word to all their friends, that should get the word out to more than she could reach alone, but still…there were so many readers out there to reach! Maybe she should look into those Amazon ads she'd heard about. After all, having Amazon show her book to their audience—especially if she had the chance to describe the audience she wanted—had to be a great way to meet new readers. And after spending so much time learning her target reader, she knew exactly how to describe them.

She added "Amazon Ads" in a circle extending from her "Advertising" bubble. Her mind began to spin with ideas. She had that list of ads she'd purchased for her first book. Some had seemed to bring in sales, while others were a bust. Popping up the excel spreadsheet where she'd kept her notes, she skimmed the list, then highlighted the ad sites she wanted to try again.

She needed more than just her experiences, though. If only she had a pool of authors to ask about their favorite advertising… Ah-ha! Flipping up her web browser, she clicked on Facebook and searched the list of groups she'd joined. There. "Authors Helping Each Other With Marketing." After her advertising efforts on her first novel, she'd watched the posts closely in this group. Authors seemed to be eager to help each other, giving actual numbers they'd spent and earned in each promotion. After skimming the recent posts, and even doing a search for "best advertising sites," she couldn't quite find what she was looking for. So, she started a new post:

> Hi guys! I'm preparing for the release of my second novel and looking for help on the best places to advertise. I plan to try Amazon's ads, but what else have you found helpful? I feel like there's so much I don't know about. Thanks in advance!

There. She sat back and released a long breath. But before the spent air had fully left her lungs, a comment popped up beneath her post.

\* \* \* \* \*

Paid ads are the third of my three can't-live-without tools on a book launch. (Remember what the other two favorites were?) When it comes to direct sales, paid advertising is hands-down one of the most effective tools to reach new readers. With the potential for good, though, comes a strong cautionary tale. To date, there are thousands of websites that offer book promotion for a price, so it's critical to be selective in your approach.

We'll cover two different types of paid advertising here, as these are most useful for book sales.

The first is:

**Targeted Email Distribution.**

The concept is simple. Readers sign up on a website to receive daily emails that feature books in the categories they select. Authors pay a fee to have their book featured in that email. Many sites also include promotion on Facebook and Twitter, along with the email distribution.

Most email distribution sites require the books they feature to be on sale, so it's best to plan your deals and coordinate them according to your pricing strategy. I'll talk more about strategy depending on your type of release in one of the bonus chapters at the end of this book.

Here are a few of the best sites currently:

- BookBub.com is by far the most successful and well-known in this category. They accept a very small number of books submitted for their daily Featured Deals emails, and the pricing isn't cheap. But don't let these factors discourage you! A BookBub feature almost always earns at least three or four times the cost of the submission, and the featured book usually rockets to the top of the bestseller list in its Amazon genre category. Which makes your books **visible** to even more readers. From there, if you've done a good job with the prerequisites (cover, description, and reviews), sales will often remain higher than usual for several weeks.

One additional note about BB: They have fairly strict requirements regarding previous sale pricing for that book, as well as cover design for box sets, and other details. Be sure to read the requirements *in detail* **several months before** you plan to submit for a Featured Deal.

- Ereadernewstoday.com
  and RobinReads.com are other sites that often do well, although not the same results as BB.

There are hundreds (possibly thousands) of other sites that offer this same targeted email marketing. Make sure you vet a potential advertiser before spending money on them. Look at the number of subscribers (especially email, not just Facebook or Twitter followers) compared to the price they charge. Also, make sure they're readership is strong in your book's genre. A particular site might provide great ROI for general market fantasy, but not so much for Christian women's fiction.

**Cost-per-Click Ads**

These are the second type of Paid Ads we'll cover, and are offered by a variety of platforms, including Facebook, Amazon, BookBub, and others.

What is it?

This concept has been around for a while, and Google AdWords is probably the most well-known venue outside of the book world. Basically, you create an ad and attach keywords to it. When a user types one of your keywords in a search field, your ad competes in a bidding war with other ads that have the same keyword. The ad that is the highest relevant bidder is shown to the user, but you are only charged your bidded price if the user clicks on your ad. Basically, you only pay if they click.

I'll quickly cover the primary CPC options for books: Facebook, Amazon (AMS), Goodreads, Google AdWords, and BookBub.

> **Facebook** has done a great job targeting ads to specific interests. I've mentioned Lead Generation ads through FB are helpful for finding your target reader while building your mailing list, but for direct sales of books, you'll want to choose "Traffic" as your marketing objective in the ad set-up. I put together a blog post[6] that walks through the steps of setting up a FB ad for book sales.
>
> A few comments about FB sales ads:
>
> - You will generally find the best ROI (return on investment) when you're running an ad for a book priced $3.99 or above. Box sets generally do very well. This also makes FB ads a good advertising tool when your book is not on sale (unlike most email advertising sites).
>
> - Make sure your ad image and text are interesting to your target reader!

[6] https://theambitiousauthor.com/2015/09/29/facebook-ads-demystified/

- You will often need to tweak various parts of the ad until you find the right combination of copy, image, interest targeting, etc. Here[7] is a blog post that can help with tweaking based on the problems you might experience.

- When your ad is doing well and you want to up your daily spend, don't ever increase the spend

### INDIE INSIGHTS

*If your book is in Kindle Unlimited through Amazon's KDP Select program, that's a great selling point to make prominent in Facebook ads. "Free in Kindle Unlimited!"*

by more than 50% at a time. The FB algorithms take a couple days to settle out with each new spend amount.

**Amazon** pay-per-click ads through Amazon Marketing Services (AMS) are the latest hot thing in author advertising. They've actually been around for several years, but it's taken Amazon a while to get the targeting right. They're still not perfect, and it's often very hard to get an ad to actually spend the daily budget you set. Currently, there are almost as many opinions on how to make these ads work as

---

[7] https://theambitiousauthor.com/2016/10/10/troubleshooting-facebook-ads/

there are books for sale on Amazon (almost). I'll try to keep my comments here to those that are generally accepted by most authors/advertisers.

Amazon offers two options: Sponsored Keyword ads show up in search results, and Product Display ads show on book pages and Kindle screens.

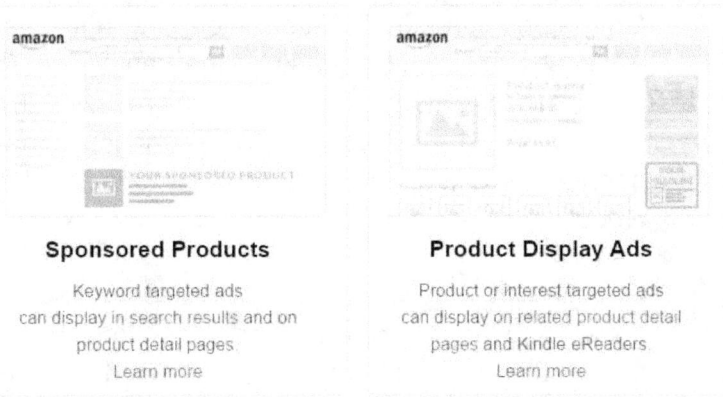

**Sponsored Products**

Keyword targeted ads can display in search results and on product detail pages. Learn more

**Product Display Ads**

Product or interest targeted ads can display on related product detail pages and Kindle eReaders. Learn more

One thing I appreciate about AMS ads are the fact that it tracks the ad performance all the way through the sales process, and actually shows you how many **book sales** were generated from clicks on your ad.

It's also fairly easy to create a campaign. You'll need to set a maximum bid amount and a total budget for the campaign. One of the most important sections is the place to enter keywords. Most people find best results from listing other authors their readers enjoy, which means this is a great place to use those comparable authors you listed when you were discovering your target reader!

**Goodreads** has a similar advertising platform, with a fairly easy set-up process. Unfortunately, many authors see few sales from a Goodreads advertising campaign. One benefit I do appreciate from GR advertising is the fact they show you how many readers have added your book to one of their GR shelves.

One other nice benefit Goodreads offers is a daily email showing the progress of the campaign. The email tells how many views the ad has received, how many clicks, how much money spent, how many people have added the book to one of their Goodreads shelves, and more.

**Google AdWords:** Google has been doing this advertising thing for years and really knows what they're doing. Despite that, I haven't used AdWords for book advertising in almost two years. The reason is that most people don't look for new books through a Google search. In terms of actual book sales, FB and Amazon have the right audiences and a whole lot of them!

**BookBub Ads (not BB Featured Deals):** This was a new opportunity that began last year, and I was thrilled to have the opportunity to use the ads platform. BookBub Ads always appear at the bottom of their daily Featured Deals emails to readers, with a real-time auction determining which ads are shown in each email.

When you create a campaign, you decide which readers you want to target and how much you're willing to pay for an impression from those audiences (one opened email = one impression). When a reader opens an email, BookBub serves the ad of the highest bidder targeting that reader at that moment.

I kept careful metrics on my ad results, and was able to maintain a positive ROI for several weeks. Unfortunately, even though BB's reader platform is huge, it's not as big as FB or Amazon. That means it's easy to saturate the audience within a few weeks. So, my recommendation for BB ads? Use them for as long as they provide good ROI, but keep a close eye.

Whew! That's all we'll cover in this section, but we've only barely scratched the surface. If you'd like to receive ongoing info or best practices from my paid advertising experiments and experiences, sign-up for alerts at http://TheAmbitiousAuthor.com.

---

### TRAD-PUBed TIPS

*Paid ads should always be part of the conversation with your publisher as you create a marketing plan together. Ask if they will cover or split the cost of any ads you agree to line up.*

*Also, you'll need to coordinate with your publisher to ensure the book will be at the correct sale price when the ad runs.*

---

# Homework

This lesson is such an important one, I have two separate homework assignments, although the first may be helpful for the second.

1.  Find and join at least one Facebook group of authors who collaborate to share marketing tips and techniques. If you are already part of a thriving community who fits this description (either on FB or through another resource), you've scored 102% on this first assignment (two bonus points for being on top of things). Proceed to assignment #2…

2.  Create a list of successful paid advertising sources, ranking them by either your own previous experience or the recommendations of other authors. To complete this list, it may be helpful to research previous posts and files in the group you joined. Even if you don't plan to utilize paid advertising as part of your book launch, having a group of resources will be very helpful in the future!

# 9

# Tool #6: Blog Tours

Kelly drifted into exhausted sleep that night, her mind weary, yet still spinning with all the ideas and things she needed to do. Emails to send. Websites to research. And she hadn't even finished filling out the "New Reader" section on her chart.

Tomorrow was another day. She could finish her plan tomorrow.

Some time later, Kelly jerked awake. She blinked, struggling to orient herself. No light filtered around the edges of the blinds, which meant it couldn't be morning yet. Still, her mind had sprung to life as if she'd slept a full night.

Guest blogs. Wouldn't it be wonderful if she could somehow get a post on that blog put together by a half dozen of her favorite authors? So many of their readers matched her target reader. But how could she ever obtain a guest post? Just contact one of the authors through their website? She didn't actually know any of them, but maybe some of her author friends might be mutual acquaintances. The worst thing they could say is no, but if she offered content interesting to their readers, it might actually be beneficial to all parties.

She sat up and grabbed her phone, pressing the home button to eliminate the screen. It would wake her too fully to turn on the light and find her notebook right now, but at least she could send herself a note so she could add this to the chart in the morning. In the message, she added the names of a few other blogs that her target readers probably followed. What a great way to introduce her books and her brand to new people.

\* \* \* \* \*

The last two tools we'll cover tend to be helpful in increasing your brand (and book) awareness. This doesn't always translate directly into book sales, so be aware of that if you choose to utilize these tools.

## Blog Tours

I often encourage a blog tour for a new author's debut release, as it gets your name and book out there in front of potential readers. A debut novel is the time to pull out all the stops, in my opinion. Kick-starting a career with momentum helps build a foundation for future releases, especially if your next release is within six to nine months of the first.

Personally, because I usually release a new book every 3-5 months, I don't do blog tours for each release. I do like to do a tour any time I release a first-in-series book, however.

When it comes to blog tours, there are really two kinds:

- **Blog visits**. These can take the form of author interviews, guest posts, or sometimes even book excerpts. A "tour" can be coordinated by the author, or you can use a professional service to coordinate with various blogs. I've done both, and both methods can be time-consuming! But you'll likely see value in keeping your name out there within your author community and their respective readership.

  As you're coordinating a blog tour, make sure you focus on blogs with the same readership as your target reader. Your time is valuable, so make sure you spend it wisely.

- **Book review tours.** These are the other type of blog tour, and these consist of bloggers who read and post reviews of the books on their blog. These can be another great source of word-of mouth-awareness, and you may see a few sales from this, as well, because avid readers follow these sites to find trusted books. Many review bloggers also post their reviews on Amazon and Goodreads, which is an added bonus (if they like your book). I'm a fan of this option, but know that a book review tour should be planned approximately 9-12 months in advance, as the reviewers need to work the books into their reading schedule. And we all know there are only 24 hours in a day!

  Again, this type of tour can be coordinated through a tour service, or you can reach out to each review blog directly to plan your own tour.

---

### TRAD-PUBed TIPS

*Many publishers send all of their books to a long list of book reviewers, often utilizing a review tour service such as litfusegroup.com. Make sure you discuss this with your publisher before taking any action on your own.*

*Also, your publisher may have a preferred connection or discount for blog tours if you plan to pursue that route. One more advantage to working with a team of industry professionals!*

---

## Homework

Jot down at least ten blogs or review services who reach your target audience. If you can't think of ten, don't cheat here! Pull up a web browser and do some research.

Even if you decide not to do a blog or review tour for this book launch, having the knowledge of sites that reach your target reader will be invaluable as you continue your writing career.

# 10

# Tool #7: Launch Parties

You've worked so hard on your book and, especially if this is your debut launch, you likely have a community of people who have cheered you through the process and can't wait to read the end result!

A launch party is a great opportunity to celebrate with your fan base. Keep in mind, you often won't see a significant number of sales from a launch party, but the value comes from the reader enthusiasm you build through the event.

Facebook is one of the most popular online platforms currently, especially with the scheduling and "Live" features.

Also, I still hear about great in-person events authors have hosted. If you're going for an in-person launch party, venues could be your local library, bookstore, or another place that already has built-in support.

A twist on combining the two would be to add a Facebook event coordinated at the same time as the in-person event, with someone assigned to head the FB portion and film as part of Facebook Live.

**Best Practices**

- Have a few giveaways! Think of themes from your book that would make great reader gifts and have fun with it! Or if you prefer to keep it simple, readers still enjoy a good gift card. I recommend not giving away a copy of your book, as that can discourage people from buying their own as they wait for the winner to be announced.
- One tip I've found to help in-person events to be successful is to put a few "influencers" in place who will lead the charge with inviting people.
- If you know of an author writing in a similar genre who also has a new release, combining efforts in a launch party (either online or local) means you can hopefully draw more readers than either of you would individually.
- For online parties, have a cohost. Someone who can take some of the pressure off you, and even keep the fun going in case of technical difficulties.
- Consider creating some discussion questions, especially for use in an online party. It gets the conversation flowing!

The decision to do a launch party and whether to host it in-person or online is entirely yours. And if you choose this route, have lots of fun with it!

# 11

# Postmortem

In the world of Project Management, a postmortem is a special meeting where the project team reconvenes after everything is complete. We talk through what went right on the project and the parts we've all tried to forget. It's a "lessons learned" session; a review so we'll all actually learn those lessons and (hopefully) not make the same mistakes on the next project. What worked? What was a waste of time? What do you want to try differently next time?

A book launch is, in itself, a project. A short-term undertaking with start and finish dates. So I love the idea of holding my own private postmortem for each book launch. As I work to make each launch more successful than the last, I can focus on areas that yield strong results and ditch the efforts that were a waste. Also, this gives me a good pulse on how book marketing is evolving.

Doing a good launch analysis requires these couple of steps:

- During your launch, keep a schedule of everything you do and how it works.

- 2-4 weeks after the launch, review your schedule and add in any missing data to show the results of each action.

- Then analyze the outcome. Your postmortem should have these sections at least:

  1. **Launch timeline:** What you did when, and the result (click rates from your email list, book ranking after key blog posts, etc.). Record this as if you'll be struck with amnesia the next time you review this document. Write down every milestone in the launch process: pricing, ads purchased, emails sent to your list, blog tours, giveaways, everything! I also like to record how many books are sold each month during the pre-order period.

  2. **What worked:** Create an exhaustive list of everything you did that worked well, both in keeping your workload down and in selling books. You'll want to do this stuff again on the next launch.

  3. **What didn't work:** Include things that either weren't helpful or actually made things worse.

  4. **What you'd like to do differently on the next launch:** For either of the two sections previous, are there activities you'd like to tweak before trying again? Maybe a software you want to try to help with automation. Or maybe a missed opportunity you didn't find until it was too late.

When you begin planning the launch for your next book, make sure you look at your postmortem notes to make this one even better than the last!

## Homework

If you've ever been part of a book release, think through that launch process and go through the postmortem process. You might find some valuable insights to add to your new launch!

# 12

# Bonus!

# Example Launch Plans

Every author and book is unique, and we all have different goals for our book releases and career paths. With that said, there tend to be general guidelines for where a launch should focus, depending on a variety of factors. I'm going to attempt to cover some of those guidelines here, keeping in mind our goal to reach both existing readers and new readers (turning them into existing readers for your next launch):

## Debut Release:

**This is the time to pull out the stops as you're introducing your book to the world and building your brand (and email list).**

- **Email List.** Have email list sign-ups everywhere you can think of, but especially in the back matter of your eBook and on your website. It would be a great idea if you had a short story or some other incentive to encourage readers to sign-up.
- **Launch Team.** Try to have at least 20-30 people lined up to post reviews the first couple of weeks. You'll find it can be easier to do this on your debut than later books because of the excitement around your budding career.

- **Blog Tour.** If you ever plan to do a blog tour, this is the time. You're building your brand and working to get your name out there, both efforts where blog tours can be helpful.

**Other options:**

- **Paid Advertising:** If you plan to utilize this, I would recommend waiting until there are at least 15 Amazon reviews on the book with a 4.6 star rating or higher, then submit to ENT and/or Robin Reads. (Make sure you coordinate with your publisher). Once you have at least 25 reviews on the book and meet the pricing requirements, begin submitting to BookBub. It may take several months of submissions to be accepted, but persevere.

- **Launch Parties:** This is entirely your choice, but there's no better time to celebrate than the release of the debut novel you've worked so hard on!

\* \* \* \* \*

## Later Book in a Series:

**It likely won't take much to encourage readers to follow you through the books in a series as they already love the characters; the hard part is finding them again to tell them about the new release. That's where the value of an email list comes in.**

- **Email List.** Utilize the email list you've been growing since your debut, by sending at least the three emails we discussed to your list. Make sure you're working to add new readers to your list, too, by having email list sign-ups everywhere you can think of - especially in the back matter of your eBook and on your website.

- **Launch Team.** It's easy to be more lax with your launch team on later books in a series, so put some focus into keeping the excitement going. Try to add more numbers to your team with each launch, knowing that not everyone will review every book.

- **Paid Advertising:**

  - Advertising the previous book in the series: During the preorder phase of your new release, consider running a sale or promotion on the series book just before the new story. You'll see an uptick in preorder sales!

  - Advertising the new release: I would recommend waiting until there are at least 15 Amazon reviews on the book with a 4.6 star rating or higher, then submit to ENT and/or

Robin Reads. (Make sure you coordinate with your publisher). Once you have at least 25 reviews on the book and meet the pricing requirements, begin submitting to BookBub. It may take several months of submissions to be accepted, but persevere.

\* \* \* \* \*

## First Book in New Series:

**You won't have the momentum of the series and familiar characters to carry your new book, so you'll want to do more outreach to spread the word and build excitement for the new series.**

- **Email List.** Utilize the email list you've been growing since your debut, by sending at least the three emails we discussed to your list. Make sure you're working to add new readers to your list, too, by having email list sign-ups everywhere you can think of—especially in the back matter of your eBook and on your website.

- **Launch Team.** Work to invigorate your launch team about the new series. Give them ARCs early, if possible, and consider providing quotes and memes for them to share on social media.

**Other options:**

- **Paid Advertising:** If you plan to utilize this, I would recommend waiting until there are at least 15 Amazon reviews on the book with a 4.6 star rating or higher, then submit to ENT and/or Robin Reads. (Make sure you coordinate with your publisher). Once you have at least 25 reviews on the book and meet the pricing requirements, begin submitting to BookBub. It may take several months of submissions to be accepted, but persevere.

- **Blog Tour.** Consider doing a blog tour (even if it's scaled down) to get the word out about the new series.

# 13

# Bonus!

# Tips to make it manageable (and keep your sanity!)

- **Keep an ongoing list of launch ideas.** Use the format that works best for you (Excel spreadsheet, paper notebook, or even a Scrivener document). Ideally, you can organize the list by category, similar to the tools listed in this book. When it's time to plan a new book launch, review your list and choose which tools will be most effective for that release.

- **Don't try to do everything.** Consider how much experience, time, and money you want to invest in this book launch, then plan accordingly.

- **Make a plan**. I've referred to this idea many times throughout the book, but let me say it plainly. When you begin planning your launch, write (or type) a clear list of the marketing activities you want to do for the new release, then assign dates to each activity. It may also help to use a calendar (either online or paper) to keep you on track.

- **Enlist friends and family.** Especially if this is your debut novel, you probably have people excited about your new release. Don't be afraid to ask for their help. If they jump at the opportunity, give them clear direction on what you'd like them to do, then let them own it!

- **Enjoy the process.** Many authors, myself included, would rather snuggle into my writing cave and brainstorm the next book, but the act of sharing your new story with the world can also be exciting! Take a moment to celebrate and enjoy the moment.

Want more book marketing insights and best practices?
Sign up at https://TheAmbitiousAuthor.com
to receive them in your inbox.

For starters, I'll send you a FREE Marketing Checklist for your next Book Launch.


\* \* \* \* \*


If this book was helpful to you, will you please consider leaving a review?
https://www.amazon.com/dp/B06XZNBHJM

As an author, you know how helpful reviews can be, *so please accept my thanks for taking that action!*

# About the Author

 **Misty M. Beller** writes Christian historical romance, and is a hybrid author of eleven novels, all of which have spent regular time on the Amazon bestselling lists.

With over ten years working in professional project management and marketing, Misty uses her experience in the corporate world to develop best practices in her writing and book marketing efforts. It is her passion to help other authors on this same journey.

Misty teaches courses and workshops at writers' conferences around the U.S., educating authors on effective book marketing approaches and helping them apply that knowledge to their own books. To schedule Misty, connect through her website:
https://theambitiousauthor.com/speaking-engagements-and-media/

www.ingramcontent.com/pod-product-compliance
Lightning Source LLC
Chambersburg PA
CBHW062016280526
45787CB00005B/2127